THE BOOK
OF
ITALIAN
WISDOM

THE BOOK OF ITALIAN WISDOM

ANTONIO SANTI

CITADEL PRESS
Kensington Publishing Corp.
www.kensingtonbooks.com

CITADEL PRESS books are published by

Kensington Publishing Corp.
850 Third Avenue
New York, NY 10022

Copyright ©2003 Red Parrot Press

All Kensington titles, imprints, and distributed lines are available at special quantity discounts for bulk purchases for sales promotions, premiums, fund-raising, educational, or institutional use. Special book excerpts or customized printings can also be created to fit specific needs. For details, write or phone the office of the Kensington special sales manager: Kensington Publishing Corp., 850 Third Avenue, New York, NY 10022, attn: Special Sales Department, phone 1-800-221-2647.

Citadel Press and the Citadel logo are trademarks of Kensington Publishing Corp.

First printing September 2003

10 9 8 7 6 5 4 3

Printed in the United States of America

ISBN 0-8065-2506-1

Library of Congress Control Number: 2003100141

To Pina and Norberto,
who showed me the real Italy

All roads lead to Rome. . . .

Contents

Preface   *xi*

Wisdom   3

Success   19

La Dolce Vita   41

Amore   55

Friendship   67

Age   75

Money   81

Art   91

Cinema   101

Music   113

La Famiglia   121

Food   135

La Mama   149

America   157

Being Italian American   171

Rabiole (Miscellany)   185

Sources   201

Preface

THE ITALIAN WAY of thinking and speaking is uniquely expressive, well matched to the lively Italian personality. Italians have expressions for everything! And many of them have become part of the American language. We all know *"Mama mia!,"* *"la dolce vita,"* and even *"in flagrante delicto."* And is there anyone who doesn't know what *caffe latte* is?

From the time of Julius Caesar in Rome to Frank Sinatra in New Jersey to modern-day Michigan-born Madonna, Italians have been quoted in literature, music, and folklore.

In a book about making friends and doing business in Italy, it is suggested to avoid bringing up religion, politics, taxes, World War II, the Mafia, and Italian stereotypes, and to refrain from criticizing Italian culture, even if your Italian counterparts are doing so. Once, giggling about the inefficiency of the Italian railroad while waiting several hours for a train to load onto the ferry to Messina in Sicily, a companion of mine was belligerently chided by an Italian friend, "Oh, and I suppose *everything* in America works *perfectly.*"

But in a book about Italian wisdom, how could we resist touching on some of these topics? Some of the pithiest quotes come from Italians and Italian Americans on things like money, family life, and being an American of Italian heritage. Of course, food is something we Italians always talk about. So are love, friendship, success, and life. Insults are an expression of wit, and we Italians can banter with the best of them.

So join me for a short journey through what makes it great to be Italian. Remember, though, like a good antipasto, it is just a tasty beginning. *Tutti a tavola!*

The BOOK
OF
ITALIAN
WISDOM

Wisdom

Proverbs

Misfortune does not always result in harm.

Don't make your children better than yourself.

He who loves you makes you cry. He who hates you makes you laugh.

When the danger is past, God is cheated.

To him who is determined it remains only to act.

If you scatter thorns, don't go barefoot.

If the secret sorrows of everyone could be read on their foreheads, how many who now cause envy would suddenly become the objects of pity.

Between saying and doing, many a pair of shoes is worn out.

Often he who does too much does too little.

He who enjoys good health is rich, though he knows it not.

Once the game is over, the king and the pawn go back in the same box.

Reason lies between the bridle and the spur.

The best armor is to keep out of range.

He who knows little knows enough if he knows how to hold his tongue.

A little man often casts a long shadow.

Voices

Do not appear to give advice, but put your view forward discreetly in conversation.

—*Giovanni di Bicci de' Medici*

I think that somehow we have to come up with something that gives us answers, maybe not true answers, but at least hypothetical propositions that might eventually lead to true answers.

—*Paolo Soleri*

Doubt is the father of invention.

I have been . . . suspected of heresy, that is, of having held and believed that the sun is the center of the universe and immovable, and that the earth is not the center of the same and that it does move . . .

I do not feel obliged to believe that the same God who has endowed us with sense, reason, and intellect has intended us to forgo their use.

—*Galileo Galilei*

First reach them, then teach them.

—*A. J. Montanari*

A man only becomes wise when he begins to calculate the approximate depth of his ignorance.

—*Gian Carlo Menotti*

Everyone is born with genius, but most people only keep it a few minutes.

—*Edgard Varese*

Men willingly believe what they wish.

—*Julius Caesar*

. . . human beings are the only ones that go over and over and do the same mistakes over and over. We never learn.

—*Jennifer Capriati*

If education is always to be conceived along the same antiquated lines of a mere transmission of knowledge, there is little to be hoped from it in the bettering of man's future. For what is the use of transmitting knowledge if the individual's total development lags behind?

The first idea the child must acquire is that of the difference between good and evil.

—*Maria Montessori*

When baseball is no longer fun it's no longer a game.

—*Joe DiMaggio*

Every human being has this outlook that we think we're in charge, and just when we start to get ahead, reality comes crashing down and we realize we're not as in charge as we think.

—*Sylvester Stallone*

The difference between a smart man and a wise man is that a smart man knows what to say, a wise man knows whether or not to say.

—*Frank M. Garafola*

There's no sense in whipping a tired horse, because he'll quit on you. More horses are whipped out of the money than into it.

—*Eddie Arcaro*

A president needs men around him who bleed when he is cut.

—*Joseph A. Califano, Jr.*

You have to leave the city of your comfort and go into the wilderness of your intuition. What you'll discover will be wonderful. What you'll discover will be yourself.

—*Alan Alda*

It is no good to try to stop knowledge from going forward. Ignorance is never better than knowledge.

—*Enrico Fermi*

Far better to think historically, to remember the lessons of the past. Thus, far better to conceive of power as consisting in part of the knowledge of when not to use all the power you have. Far better to be one who knows that if you reserve the power not to use all your power, you will lead others far more successfully and well.

—*A. Bartlett Giamatti*

We must create an atmosphere where the crooked cop fears the honest cop, and not the other way around.

—*Frank Serpico*

My philosophy? Man is a little bit better than his reputation, and a little bit worse.

—*Al Pacino*

I am,
Indeed,
A king,
Because I know how
To rule myself.

—*Pietro Aretino*

Power tires only those who do not have it.

—*Giulio Andreotti*

A fair request should be followed by the deed in silence.

A great flame follows a little spark.

He who sees a need and waits to be asked for help is as unkind as if he had refused it.

—*Dante Alighieri*

A hunch is creativity trying to tell you something.

—*Frank Capra*

You don't have to have fought in a war to love peace.

—*Geraldine A. Ferraro*

He who doesn't fear death dies only once.

—*Giovanni Falcone*

Never tell everything at once.

—Ken Venturi

In the fight between you and the world, back the world.

—Frank Zappa

All armed prophets have been victorious, and all unarmed prophets have been destroyed.

A prince never lacks legitimate reasons to break his promise.

Benefits should be conferred gradually; and in that way they will taste better.

—Niccolò Machiavelli

Why must we always milk the public goat and never touch the sacred cow?

—Mario Procaccino

Law feeds and is fed by the world around it.

—*Judge Guido Calabresi*

It's better to destroy than create what's unnecessary.

—*from the film 8 1/2*

If you would fain by worthy deeds be known,
Seek to be prisoned without cause, lie long,
And find no friend to listen to your moan.

—*Benvenuto Cellini*

A man who lives everywhere lives nowhere.

Conceal a flaw, and the world will imagine the worst.

—*Marcus Valerius Martialis*

No man is wise enough by himself.

—*Titus Maccius Plautus*

The best plan is to profit by the folly of others.

—*Pliny the Elder*

Fundamentally, humility is not a quality that exists in people. It is something only between a person and his God. What people consider "humble" is actually good manners. Good manners is the bottom line.

—*Julius La Rosa*

Man is only miserable so far as he thinks himself so.

—*Jacopo Sannazaro*

Start by doing what's necessary, then do what's possible, and suddenly you are doing the impossible.

Where there is patience and humility, there is neither anger nor vexation.

While you are proclaiming peace with your lips, be careful to have it even more fully in your heart.

—*St. Francis of Assisi*

I have not told half of what I saw.

—*Marco Polo*

I have come to believe that the whole world is an enigma, a harmless enigma that is made terrible by our own mad attempt to interpret it as though it had an underlying truth.

—*Umberto Eco*

In the circle in which I travel, a dumb man is more dangerous than a hundred rats.

—*Joe Valachi*

I love those who can smile in trouble, who can gather strength from distress, and grow brave by reflection. 'Tis the business of little minds to shrink, but they whose heart is firm, and whose conscience approves their conduct, will pursue their principles unto death.

—*Leonardo da Vinci*

Never get angry. Never make a threat. Reason with people.

—*Mario Puzo*

Success

Proverbs

A little man often casts a long shadow.

Chi esce riesce [He who leaves succeeds].

Of the wealth of the world each has as much as they take.

Those who make themselves sheep will be eaten by the wolf.

One who sleeps doesn't catch fish.

It is not enough to aim; you must hit.

Be content to remain what your father was. Then you'll be neither a knave nor an ass.

Voices

I'll take any way to get into the Hall of Fame. If they want a batboy, I'll go in as a batboy.

—*Phil Rizzuto*

A ball player's got to be kept hungry to become a big leaguer. That's why no boy from a rich family ever made it to the big leagues.

—*Joe DiMaggio*

In order to succeed you must fail, so that you know what not to do the next time.

—*Anthony J. D'Angelo*

I have worked without thinking of myself. This [is] the largest factor in whatever success I have attained.

—*A. P. Giannini*

Whosoever desires constant success must change his conduct with the times.

No enterprise is more likely to succeed than one concealed from the enemy until it is ripe for execution.

—Niccolò Machiavelli

Getting ahead in a difficult profession requires avid faith in yourself. That is why some people with mediocre talent, but with great inner drive, go much farther than people with vastly superior talent.

—Sophia Loren

Those of us who didn't hit quick with one record had time to survive a series of misfortunes and starvation. By the time we were lucky and made it, we were pros.

—Frankie Laine

Western civilization, unfortunately, does not link knowledge and morality but, rather, it connects knowledge and power and makes them equivalent.

—Vine Deloria, Jr.

I get to sing whatever I want and paint whatever I want, and enjoy the freedom that every artist wants.

—*Tony Bennett*

Style is knowing who you are, what you want to say, and not giving a damn.

—*Gore Vidal*

I don't ever have to worry about this business going to pot. There's always going to be cemeteries, no question about it.

—*Raymond Bocci*

Everyone is proud of his own family name, but sacrifices are necessary for progress.

—*Chef Hector Boiardi on changing his company name to Boy-Ar-Dee*

I would rather lose people than lose the city.

—*Cosimo Medici*

My first qualification for this great office is my monumental personal ingratitude. You can't be a good mayor and a good fellow.

—*Fiorello La Guardia*

It never was my ambition to run the biggest winery in the world. It doesn't impress me at all.

—*Julio Gallo*

The real hero is always a hero by mistake; he dreams of being an honest coward like everybody else.

—*Umberto Eco*

Rocky turned out to be kind of a metaphor for everyone's struggle. It wasn't about me, Sylvester Stallone, and money. It was just about wanting to fail on your own terms. It was about wanting a chance at failure; Rocky never thought he'd succeed. But like him, I just wanted to try.

—*Sylvester Stallone*

A man has to be good good or bad bad to be remembered.

—*Simon Rodia*

I was always nervous no matter how many times I sang a role. I took some comfort in knowing that Caruso, even though world famous, became nervous before every performance.

—*Rosa Ponselle*

Confidence is contagious. So is lack of confidence.

If winning isn't everything, why do they keep score?

—*Vince Lombardi*

The greatest sign of success for a teacher . . . is to be able to say, "The children are now working as if I did not exist."

—*Maria Montessori*

You can get much farther with a kind word and a gun than you can with a kind word alone.

—Al Capone

I've done nothing that I can call exciting. I was a barber. Since then I've been a singer. That's it.

—Perry Como

No matter what business you're in, you can't run in place or someone will pass you by. It doesn't matter how many games you've won.

It took me a long time to learn that the relationship between hard work and success is NOT direct. If you work hard, you'll be successful; that is not the case. The relationship is: If you don't work hard, then you can't be successful.

Be a dreamer. If you don't know how to dream, you're dead.

—Jimmy Valvano

I owe [Arthur] Godfrey. Being fired was the greatest thing that could have happened to me.

—Julius LaRosa

You can succeed without winning. . . . To me, success is playing—or working—to the best of your ability.

—*Joe Torre*

✤

If you want to please the critics, don't play too loud, too soft, too fast, too slow.

—*Arturo Toscanini*

✤

Mickey Mouse . . . is always there—he's part of my life. That really is something not everyone can call their claim to fame.

I owe everything to those ears.

—*Annette Funicello*

✤

Virtue herself is her own fairest reward.

—*Silius Italicus*

✤

Once I played with a baseball team that was so bad, we'd have a victory celebration when the game was rained out.

—*Joe Gargiola*

Success? It's not five million dollars. I'd call it contentment. It's your being contented and your family being contented.

—Frank Fontaine

Coming to America changed my life to a greater extent than I thought possible. From a dreamy, lazy boy, I became almost overnight an aggressive and determined man—determined to succeed.

—Pietro Belluschi

My real friends and my family know that if I'm not working I'm miserable. It's not for monetary reasons. I already have fame and fortune. Now I want to find the greatness in things—which is why I was attracted to the arts in the first place.

—Jon Bon Jovi

Once in a man's life, for one mortal moment, he must make a grab for immortality; if not, he has not lived.

—Sylvester Stallone

I had reached a lifetime goal: Making something out of nothing; a nobody became Mr. Somebody—and I made the world like it. . . . Marquee lights featured "Frank Capra" above the title of the film and the names of the stars—the first hired director to wrest that distinction from the Hollywood Establishment.

—*Frank Capra*

Creativity is a certain delusion. It's really a matter of chance and luck and a certain energy in facing difficulties.

—*Salvador E. Luria*

Every now and then, go away, have a little relaxation, for when you come back to your work your judgment will be surer since to remain constantly at work will cause you to lose power of judgment.

I have offended God and mankind because my work didn't reach the quality it should have.

Even the richest soil, if left uncultivated, will produce the rankest weeds.

—*Leonardo da Vinci*

I don't like to watch my own movies—I fall asleep in my own movies.

—*Robert De Niro*

Desire is the key to motivation, but it's determination and commitment to an unrelenting pursuit of your goal—a commitment to excellence—that will enable you to attain the success you seek.

—*Mario Andretti*

The Depression was the greatest thing that ever happened to me. It made me realize that there was opportunity out there if I really worked, built my luck on hard work and dedication. Is there any limit to what people can do if they set their minds to it?

—*Jeno Paulucci*

There's such a uniqueness to it, the machine kind of took on a character of its own. My father was always surprised at that. If our name had been Smith or Brown, I don't think any of this would have happened.

—*Richard Zamboni*

Know how to listen, and you will profit even from those who talk badly.

—*Plutarch*

I try to do what I know will please the audiences. What pleases me is unimportant. I didn't buy a ticket.

I would like to be known not for the heights I have reached, but for the depths from which I have risen.

—*Connie Francis*

Small projects need much more help than great.

—*Dante Alighieri*

I'd do it legal. I learned too late that you need just as good a brain to make a crooked million as an honest million. These days you apply for a license to steal from the public. If I had my time again, I'd make sure I got that license first.

Guys always told me later that I should've put my brains to runnin' a legit business and I'd have been a tremendous success. But I wouldn't've enjoyed it like what I was doin'.

—*Lucky Luciano*

I would rather be first in a little Iberian village than second in Rome.

—*Julius Caesar*

You must sacrifice, train, do everything possible to put yourself in a position to win. But if you consider second or third a failure, I feel sorry for you.

—*Joe Falcon*

We are continually faced by great opportunities brilliantly disguised as insoluble problems.

—*Lee Iacocca*

Fame is only good for one thing—they will cash your check in a small town.

—*Truman Capote*

I come to win.

—*Leo Durocher*

But for a working guy to grab a bit of knowledge in this society, it's a rough ball game. If you've got anything on the ball you end up as a little-time gangster, a racketeer.

—*Ralph Fasanella*

Never in our full life could we hope to do such work for tolerance, for justice, for man's understanding of man as now we do by accident.

—*Bartolomeo Vanzetti*

I'm excited by politics, but I wouldn't want to be president. I don't think even President Bush wants to be president. Whenever you see him on television, the expression on his face says, "This sucks. Why did I let my dysfunctional family get me into this?"

—*Janeane Garofalo*

My goal is to be remembered as a human being and as a great performer.

—*Bobby Darin*

When you build bridges you can keep crossing them.

—*Rick Pitino*

When a jockey retires, he becomes just another little man.

—*Eddie Arcaro*

It's a sign of mediocrity when you demonstrate gratitude with moderation.

—*Roberto Benigni*

One day I went to Coney Island and I had a very pretty girl with me. We were sitting on the sand. A big, husky lifeguard, maybe there were two of them, kicked sand in my face. I couldn't do anything and the girl felt funny. I told her that someday, if I meet this guy, I will lick him.

—*Charles Atlas*

The last thing in the world I thought I would be is a U.S. congressman, given all the bobcat vests and Eskimo boots I used to wear.

—*Sonny Bono*

There are occasions when it is undoubtedly better to incur loss than to make gain.

—*Titus Maccius Plautus*

At least in my time, I grew up uh . . . you had to . . . you . . . kind of . . . averted ambition. It was . . . it had a kind of pejorative connotation, for some reason. Ambition was uh . . . was negative. I don't believe that, but I do . . . do see that ambition is relative.

—*Al Pacino*

Don't you understand? Leadership isn't a multiple-choice test on the issues. Any idiot can study and pass that. Leadership is making the people feel confident in you. Leadership is setting the tone of compassion and working together and respect for the rule of law.

—*Mario Cuomo*

I was exactly where I wanted to be. I had a band. I knew who I was. We were getting work. The album reflects that. On the new record, I don't know who I am. You see, about five months after E Street came out, there was this big burst of attention from the press. Suddenly, I was the future of rock 'n' roll.

—*Bruce Springsteen*

It is not enough to succeed. Others must fail.

—*Gore Vidal*

My biggest concern during a race is getting bored. The biggest thing I have to combat is falling asleep while going around and around.

—*Mario Andretti*

The goal I seek is to have people refine their style through my clothing without having them become victims of fashion.

—*Giorgio Armani*

People underestimate me, but I've always been a stretch runner. If people would take a look—and I don't mean this arrogantly—if they would take a look at what I've done in my life, you can't be a dummy and have the achievements I've had in my lifetime.

—*Sonny Bono*

I've sung for royalty, in palaces, around the world. I've sung at the White House for Eisenhower, Johnson, Nixon, Reagan three times, Bush. Just having never gotten my diploma always stuck in my craw. Not having it makes you feel your self-esteem isn't where it should be.

—*Vic Damone*

The difference between the impossible and the possible lies in a person's determination.

[Joe DiMaggio] was the kind of guy that exemplified what a major leaguer should be like, and act like, and play like. . . . He played the game with so much intensity. He played the game with pride. He wore the Yankee uniform with dignity and character.

—*Tommy Lasorda*

If people only knew how hard I work to gain my mastery, it wouldn't seem so wonderful at all.

—*Michelangelo Buonarroti*

You have to remember that about seventy percent of the horses running don't want to win. Horses are like people. Everybody doesn't have the aggressiveness or ambition to knock himself out to become a success.

—*Eddie Arcaro*

People seem to think that I'm this charismatic, flamboyant guy. They want me to be more animated. But I don't feel comfortable getting into it.

—*Mike Piazza*

Avoid litigation and political controversy, and always keep out of the public eye.

—*Giovanni di Bicci de' Medici*

I don't believe you have to be better than everybody else. I believe you have to be better than you ever thought you could be.

—*Ken Venturi*

A big chest, a big mouth, ninety percent memory, ten percent intelligence, lots of hard work, and something in the heart.

With a beautiful voice it is not hard to reach the top. But to stay there, that is hard.

—*Enrico Caruso*

Initially, I sold the baths one at a time at county fairs and trade shows. My family was skeptical at first, until the orders steadily increased. I knew I had tapped into a great opportunity.

—*Roy Jacuzzi*

Success is a public word. No one here thinks, "Oh, if I do well in this part it will make me famous or successful." What we think about is learning it correctly, doing it, putting yourself into it.

—Kay Mazzo

It is much easier to sing well than to have to explain why you didn't sing well.

—Licia Albanese

Success came too early, too fast, and there was too much. I went from coffee money to $5,000 a week before I was twenty and I didn't handle it well.

—Vic Damone

La Dolce Vita

Proverbs

Every medal has its other side.

Don't make a step longer than your leg.

A runaway monk never praises his monastery.

At a dangerous passage, yield to precedence.

He that will not strive in this world should not have come into it.

Voices

In life nobody really understands you. The only thing you can wish for is somebody to accept you and love you for what you are.

Life is here only to be lived so that we can, through life, earn the right to death, which to me is paradise. Whatever it is that will bring me the reward of paradise, I'll do the best I can.

I was at a point where I was ready to say I am what I am because of what I am and if you like me I'm grateful, and if you don't, what am I going to do about it?

—*Anne Bancroft*

If life doesn't offer a game worth playing, then invent a new one.

—*Anthony J. D'Angelo*

Confidence is a very fragile thing.

—*Joe Montana*

I hate mankind, for I think myself one of the best of them, and I know how bad I am.

—*Joseph Baretti*

In life there are no problems, that is, objective and external choices; there is only the life which we do not resolve as a problem but which we live as an experience, whatever the final result may be.

—*Alberto Moravia*

What have I been qualified for in my life? I haven't been qualified to be a mayor. I'm not qualified to be a songwriter. I'm not qualified to be a TV producer. I'm not qualified to be a successful businessman. And so, I don't know what *qualified* means.

—*Sonny Bono*

Do you know what I especially like to do? On a hot summer night I like to put organ music on the stereo and go out in the moonlight and take a swim in my pool. As I float along on my back, I can look up and see the stars and the outline of my peacocks against the sky as they rest in the branches of my oak tree.

—*August Sebastiani*

Many untoward things can I remember, such as happen to all who live upon our earth; and from those adversities I am now more free than at any previous period of my career—nay, it seems to me that I enjoy greater content of soul and health of body than ever I did in bygone years. I can also bring to mind some pleasant goods and some inestimable evils, which, when I turn my thoughts backward, strike terror in me, and astonishment that I should have reached this age of fifty-eight, wherein, thanks be to God, I am still traveling prosperously forward.

—Benvenuto Cellini

It is not these well-fed long-haired men that I fear, but the pale and the hungry-looking.

—Julius Caesar

Once in the racket you're always in it.

—Al Capone
(Quoted in the Philadelphia Public Ledger, *1929)*

You live by the gun and knife, and die by the gun and knife.

—Joe Valachi

The principal occupation of my life has been the cultivation of the pleasures of the senses . . .

—*Giacomo Casanova*

&

All the pessimists in world history together are nothing against reality.

—*Elias Canetti*

&

There's no forgiveness in nature.

—*Ugo Betti*

&

When neither their property nor their honor is touched, the majority of men live content.

Men are so simple and yield so readily to the desires of the moment that he who will trick will always find another who will suffer to be tricked.

—*Niccolò Machiavelli*

&

Often the test of courage is not to die but to live.

—*Vittorio Alfieri*

My education was [listening to records at night] and that taught me the most important thing . . . that there's more to life than what you see around. And that was something they couldn't teach me in school, you couldn't learn it in the house, and you couldn't learn it from people you were hanging with on the street or anything. That was the most important lesson of my life. I guess at night that's the only thing we try to say. It's the only message: don't sell yourself short.

—*Bruce Springsteen*

I'm not trying to prove anybody wrong, I'm just trying to prove something to myself.

—*Mike Piazza*

Life is pretty simple: You do some stuff. Most fails. Some works. You do more of what works. If it works big, others quickly copy it. Then you do something else. The trick is the doing something else.

—*Leonardo da Vinci*

There is no greater sorrow
Than to be mindful of the happy time
In misery.

—*Dante Alighieri*

There's two possible outcomes: if the result confirms the hypothesis, then you've made a discovery. If the result is contrary to the hypothesis, then you've made a discovery.

If I could remember the names of all these particles, I'd be a botanist.

—*Enrico Fermi*

I've learned that everyday is a new day, a whole new attack to meet head on. . . .

It's a one-time shot, this life, and you don't get any second chances . . .

—*Bobby Darin*

The longest part of the journey is said to be the passing of the gate.

—*Marcus Terentius Varro*

This is the epitaph I want on my tomb: "Here lies one of the most intelligent animals who ever appeared on the face of the earth."

—*Benito Mussolini*

Lucky, very lucky. I'm talking about my whole life, not merely my professional career.

—*Julius La Rosa*

There is no end. There is no beginning. There is only the infinite passion of life.

—*Frederico Fellini*

Other people go to the office. I get to coach. I know I've been blessed.

Don't give up, don't ever give up.

—*Jimmy Valvano*

Life is, after all, essentially absurd, and I think that by working you have less time to think about that.

—*Alan Alda*

I think there are some players born to play ball.

—*Joe DiMaggio*

❧

The impermanence of fame, the way people fade in large cities that once adored them, and how little of what we do survives us.

—*Gay Talese*

❧

If everything seems under control, you're just not going fast enough.

The crashes people remember, but drivers remember the near misses.

Circumstances may cause interruptions and delays, but never lose sight of your goal. Prepare yourself in every way you can by increasing your knowledge and adding to your experience, so that you can make the most of opportunity when it occurs.

—*Mario Andretti*

❧

There is more stupidity than hydrogen in the universe, and it has a longer shelf life.

—*Frank Zappa*

❧

It is only when I am doing my work that I feel truly alive.

Unfortunately, because of our goal-oriented training, we Westerners have a vision of ourselves living through a continuous time line that requires steps, changes, conclusions, and a goal one must reach.

—*Federico Fellini*

Be nice to people on your way up because you meet them on your way down.

—*Jimmy Durante*

I never think of the future. I try to take care of the present and leave the future to God.

—*Alan Alda*

Communism doesn't work because people like to own stuff.

It isn't necessary to imagine the world ending in fire or ice; there are two other possibilities: one is paperwork, and the other is nostalgia.

—*Frank Zappa*

Reality is something you rise above.

—Liza Minnelli

❧

Victory has a hundred fathers, but defeat is an orphan.

—Count Galleazzo Ciano

❧

The greatest lesson in life is to know that even fools are right sometimes.

—Leonardo da Vinci

❧

The Mouse Club was the happiest time of my life. I know people think this is goody-goody. They say "Annette, you're sugar-coating it. It couldn't have been that good." But it really was the happiest days of my life.

—Annette Funicello

❧

Quit? Me? Not as long as there's a crab or salmon around. Where am I going to go? What do I do now?

—Frank Pomilia

❧

Amore

Proverbs

He who is not impatient is not in love.

Behind every great man there is a great woman.

Wine, women, and tobacco reduce one to ashes.

Love rules without rules.

The husband reigns, but it is the wife that governs.

Choose neither a woman nor linen by candlelight.

Without jealousy there is no love.

At the end, every flower loses its perfume.

Bed is the poor man's opera.

The bashful hog eats no pears.

Voices

There are more love songs than anything else. If songs could make you do something we'd all love one another.

—*Frank Zappa*

Love is the word used to label the sexual excitement of the young, the habituation of the middle-aged, and the mutual dependence of the old.

—*John Ciardi*

It is better to be feared than loved, if you cannot be both.

—*Niccolò Machiavelli*

The demands of my career come ahead of everything else. I have a violent temper. No woman would ever put up with that.

—*Cesare Siepi*

He loves but little who
Can say and count in words, how much he loves.

—*Dante Alighieri*

When I was very young, I kissed my first woman and smoked my first cigarette on the same day. Believe me, never since have I wasted any more time on tobacco.

—*Arturo Toscanini*

No one ever filed for divorce on a full stomach.

—*Mama Leone*

Perfect love is rare indeed—for to be a lover will require that you continually have the subtlety of the very wise, the flexibility of the child, the sensitivity of the artist, the understanding of the philosopher, the acceptance of the saint, the tolerance of the scholar, and the fortitude of the certain.

Don't hold to anger, hurt, or pain. They steal your energy and keep you from love.

—Leo Buscaglia

Many times a man has come in saying he's dining with his wife and I take him to his old wife instead of his new one.

—Vincent Sardi, Jr.

This is the way I look at sex scenes: I have basically been doing them for a living for years. Trying to seduce an audience is the basis of rock 'n' roll. And if I may say so, I'm pretty good at it. . . . Plus, being married and monogamous, it's the closest thing I can do to having sex without getting in trouble for it. . . . The only thing I like more than my wife is my money. And I'm not about to lose that to her and her lawyers, that's for damn sure.

—Jon Bon Jovi

When it comes to bed, there's no difference between a poet, a priest, or a communist!

—*Donna Rosa in* Il Postino

The soundtrack to *Indecent Exposure* is a romantic mix of music that I know most women love to hear, so I never keep it far from me when women are nearby.

—*Fabio*

There's nothing better than good sex. But bad sex? A peanut butter and jelly sandwich is better than bad sex.

—*Billy Joel*

To me, there is no greater act of courage than being the one who kisses first.

—*Janeane Garofalo*

I respect a woman too much to marry her.

—*Sylvester Stallone*

With Romeo and Juliet, you're talking about two people who meet one night, and get married the same night. I believe in love at first sight—but it hasn't happened to me yet.

—Leonardo DiCaprio

But I, and I'm embarrassed to share this confidence, I have to confess that I've never identified myself with excesses of passion and love. I seem never to have been in love in that sense. I don't understand the desperation of love as an irreparable loss.

—Federico Fellini

Teenage boys, goaded by their surging hormones . . . run in packs. They have only a brief season of exhilarating liberty between control by their mothers and control by their wives.

—Camille Paglia

Love found my all disarmed and found the way
Was clear to reach my heart down through the eyes
Which have become the halls and doors of tears.

—Petrarch

As you get older and you've been with different kinds of men, you start to recognize their types. You understand, Oh, he's one of those.

There are different phases love can have. It took me a long time to understand that forgiveness of yourself and others is something that has to be worked at. When you're younger, love just hits you. But then it gets sticky and you don't necessarily have the tools to get to the next place. Maybe you shouldn't; maybe it's designed so that you sample a lot of things, so you can shift through to your priority.

—*Susan Sarandon*

Age does not protect you from love, but love to some extent protects you from age.

—*Cornelius Tacitus*

Men are by nature fond of novelty.

—*Pliny the Elder*

When the stars make you drool
Just like pasta fazool,
That's *amore*.

> —*Dean Martin in* The Caddy,
> *from "That's Amore," by Harry Warren*

The whistling elevator man he knowing
The winking bellboy knowing
Everybody knowing! I'd almost be inclined not to do anything!

> —*Gregory Corso*

Friendship

Proverbs

Better to be alone than to be poorly accompanied.

Do not use a hatchet to remove a fly from your friend's forehead.

The friend is like the umbrella; when it's raining you never find it.

Old friends, like old wine, are best.

Voices

Sometimes the enemy of my enemy is my friend.

—*Robert G. Torricelli*

Mistakes, even occasional incompetence, could be understood and forgiven, but not disloyalty.

—*Joseph A. Califano, Jr.*

My father taught me many things . . . keep your friends close, but your enemies closer.

Friendship is everything. Friendship is more than talent. It is more than government. It is almost the equal of family.

—*from* The Godfather

A single rose can be my garden . . . a single friend, my world.

—Leo Buscaglia

Since there is nothing so well worth having as friends, never lose a chance to make them.

—Francesco Guicciardini

A man must not forget the favors gotten from a less important friend when he becomes the friend of a more important one.

—Dante Alighieri

To be honest, what I like best about golf is the camaraderie, spending time with friends.

—Bobby Rydell

The most terrible poverty is loneliness and the feeling of being unloved.

—Cornelius Tacitus

I don't go to anybody for advice about anything that's really personal. But I do have girlfriends I can talk to about what is going on. That, for me, is like therapy.

—*Susan Sarandon*

If you have to kiss somebody at 7 A.M. "on the set," you'd better be friends.

—*Sophia Loren*

Your real friends hang in there, no matter what.

—*Jerry Vale*

The number of guests at dinner should not be less than the number of the Graces nor exceed that of the Muses, i.e., it should begin with three and stop at nine.

—*Marcus Terentius Varro*

I first met Caruso during that audition [at the Riverside Theater]. He had come to hear these singing sisters. . . . When he entered the room, he walked diagonally across and spoke to me as if I were one of his own. We took to each other from the moment we met . . .

—*Rosa Ponselle*

No guest is so welcome in a friend's house that he will not become a nuisance after three days.

Nothing is there more friendly to a man than a friend in need.

—*Titus Maccius Plautus*

Popularity has a bright side, it unlocks many doors. But the truth is that I don't like it very much because it changes the private life into a very small thing.

—*Gina Lollabrigida*

I keep my friends as misers do their treasure, because, of all the things granted us by wisdom, none is greater or better than friendship.

—*Pietro Aretino*

Age

Proverbs

There is a cure for everything except death.

An old flag is an honor to the capital.

He that at twenty is not, at thirty knows not, and at forty has not, will never be, nor ever know, nor ever have.

An old chicken makes good broth.

Voices

Old injuries caught up with me, and brought on new ones. I found that it was a chore for me to straighten up after I had retrieved a ground ball. In short, I was not pleased with myself any longer, and all the fun had gone out of playing the game.

—*Joe DiMaggio*

They had people come from all over—I mean Germany . . . just to take pictures of Borgnine does it again on a horse. They said, "When you gonna get on the horse?" I said, "Bring the horse." They brought the horse. I said, "Get me a stepladder." I climbed the stepladder and got on the horse. What do you want from me? At eighty-four you don't horse around.

—*Ernest Borgnine*

Please don't retouch my wrinkles. It took me too long to earn them.

—*Anna Magnani*

I am a little stolid. I don't ride on motorcycles at ninety mph, grow orchids, or smoke marijuana.

—Alfred Drake

You never replace a great scholar who retires. If you try to do that, you end up with burnt-out volcanoes.

—Judge Guido Calabresi on A. Bartlett Giamatti's
retirement as president of Yale

Clipping coupons gives you calluses on the brain. I work because I still have the ability to create.

—Bruno Paglia

When you reach a certain age—especially at fifty, for a man—this is the crossroads time. This is the last call—"All Aboard!"—to get off this train and switch to another one. I am appreciating life much more now.

—Sylvester Stallone

On my last birthday, a friend asked me what it meant for me to be seventy, and my spontaneous response was, "Seventy? It seems to me I've always been seventy!"

—*Federico Fellini*

Old gamblers never die—they just fade and fade and fade.

—*Willie Moretti*

All men of whatsoever quality they be, who have done anything of excellence, or which may properly resemble excellence, ought, if they are persons of truth and honesty, to describe their life with their own hand; but they ought not to attempt so fine an enterprise till they have passed the age of forty.

—*Benvenuto Cellini*

I didn't write earlier because old age makes writing very difficult. There is nothing new. Now is not the time to visit because I'm in a situation where this would only add to my problems.

—*Michelangelo Buonarroti, to his nephew*

Money

Proverbs

Better a mouse in the pot than no flesh at all.

Better give a penny than lend twenty.

Public money is like holy water; people help themselves.

Steal a little, go to jail; steal a lot, make a career of it.

He who is afraid of the devil does not grow rich.

Voices

Money to get power, power to protect money.

—*Medici family motto*

I am a sensitive writer, actor, and director. Talking business disgusts me. If you want to talk business, talk to my calmly disgusting personal manager.

—*Sylvester Stallone*

We at Chrysler borrow money the old-fashioned way. We pay it back.

High interest rates are the cruelest taxes of all.

The trick is to make sure you don't die waiting for prosperity to come.

—*Lee Iacocca*

I wanted to make a lot of money, and so I let them play me up as a lounge lizard, a soft, handsome devil whose only sin in life was to sit around and be admired by women.

—*Rudolph Valentino*

We did mostly burglaries and stealing cars. We did cars for their parts or to be shipped out of the country. We never burglarized homes. That was against what we wanted to do. It was all commercial places. We'd break in at night, robbing clothing stores, hardware stores, stuff like that. We'd hold up jewelry stores, you know, with ski masks on. They all had insurance.

—*Sammy Gravano*

Thank you for making me nouveau riche.

—*Jerry Della Femina*

The time to go ahead in business is when the other fellows aren't doing much.

Our conception of a bank is that of a great public servant, an institution run in the interest of and for the welfare of the people it serves.

Money itch is a bad thing. I never had that trouble.

—*A. P. Giannini*

Avoid falsehood like the plague except in matters of taxation, which do not count, since here you are not lying to take someone else's goods, but to prevent your own from being unjustly seized.

—*Giovanni Morelli*

The Godfather is not as good as the preceding two [novels]. I wrote it to make money.

—*Mario Puzo*

I spend my days supervising the construction of St. Peter's. The Vatican's financial superintendent keeps harassing me for a progress report. My response: your lordship, I am not obliged to, nor do I intend to, tell you anything. Your job is to keep the money rolling in, and out of the hands of thieves. I will see to the building.

You wrote me a tract as long as a Bible over a triviality only to annoy me. About the money, the money [sic], please just write to me about what needs to be done. Just work it out between yourselves and spend it on what you need most.

I'm still in a fix because I haven't had a cent from this Pope in a year and I can't really ask him for anything as my work doesn't deserve it as it's not going very well. That's the trouble with this work. It's not my profession. I'm wasting my time without a good result.

—*Michelangelo Buonarroti, to his father*

I'm a gambler. Once it cost me two thousand dollars to walk across the Sands Hotel casino in Las Vegas to buy a newspaper.

—*Tony Martin*

The budget evolved from a management tool into an obstacle to management.

—Frank Carlucci

I meet some friends. They tell me money is to be made in the fish business. So I stay. I buy fish on Fisherman's Wharf. I work to buy and catch fish on the Sacramento River.

—Achille Paladini

I was in more damn political fights at the beginning. But I was fighting for a cause, and I had the people with me. Now well, if I have any enemies left, I love 'em.

—*John Brucato*

You can't kiss an oil well.

—*Joseph J. DioGuardi*

When I was a kid and a member of a real minority called a "dago" and a "wop," I felt disadvantaged . . . I can't think of a better way to pay America back.

—*Jeno Paulucci*

A lot of people will say you can make anything beautiful if you have enough money. To that I can only reply that I've been in some "great mansions" where my only reaction was you can make anything ugly if you have enough money.

—*Liberace*

It's more difficult getting up early in the morning when you're wearing silk pajamas.

—*Eddie Arcaro*

I fell never to rise to be the same man again either as a person or a talent . . . I lost my nerve . . . for fear of losing a few bucks.

—*Frank Capra*

If we ran out of money, we just went out and hijacked a truck.

—*Henry*
in the film Goodfellas

Art

Proverb

Don't pass judgment on a work of art if you don't know how to create it.

Voices

How from age to age the art of painting continually declines and deteriorates when painters have no other standard than work already done.

—*Leonardo da Vinci*

Basically, I no longer work for anything but the sensation I have while working.

—*Alberto Giacometti*

I'm very physical minded. Brain, fine, but this body is put here for use. If anybody could jump around like my heroes, it's me. Not many artists are physical types. I've been jumped on by twenty guys in a movie theater and got out alive.

—*Frank Frazetta*

If my rough hammer makes human forms out of the hard stone, it is only because of He who urges and guides its action. Only one divine being lives in Heaven and He creates beauty without human help.

I am here in great distress and with great physical strain, and have no friends of any kind, nor do I want them; and I do not have enough time to eat as much as I need; my joy and my sorrow/my repose are these discomforts.

Many believe—and I believe—that I have been designated for this work by God. In spite of my old age, I do not want to give it up; I work out of love for God, and I put all my hope in Him.

—*Michelangelo Buonarroti*

Blowing smoke rings while smoking a cigar, I observed the smoke turning and spinning on itself. It's a vortex. In the process of becoming this smoke ring, and then bifurcating and dissolving, a lot of interesting things happen, and beautiful, fluid forms are created. It's a nice image, both to look at and work with.

—*Frank Stella*

I think the Greek God as shown in the old sculptures is so splendid to look at that to be likened to one is the highest compliment that could be paid me. It was from the old sculptures that I got my first ambition to develop myself because they seemed to me to show man in his perfection.

—*Charles Atlas*

There is no limit to beauty, no saturation point in design, no end to the materials a shoemaker may use to decorate his creations so that every woman may be shod like a princess and a princess may be shod like a fairy queen.

—*Salvatore Ferragamo*

Once, I asked my father why a painter makes paintings. He said, "When a painter is hungry, he paints an apple so he can eat the apple and be satisfied." I thought it was such a marvelous thing. I had to be a painter.

—*Sandro Chia*

This tale of my sore-trouble life I write,
To thank the God of nature, who conveyed
My soul to me, and with such care hath stayed . . .
Such grace worth beauty be through me displayed
That few can rival, none surpass me quite.

—*Benvenuto Cellini*

Botticelli drew frequently, to such an extent that artists went to considerable lengths after his death to follow his drawings.

—*Giorgio Vasari*

The fountain is my speech. The tulips are my speech. The grass and trees are my speech.

—*George T. Delacorte*

Poetry doesn't belong to those who write it; it belongs to those who need it.

—*Mario Ruoppolo,*
in Il Postino

I am obsessed these days by sculpture! I think I can perceive a complete renewal of this mummified art.

—*Umberto Boccioni*

My paintings smell of oil and garlic and salami and some people just don't smell anything.

—*Ralph Fasanella*

Art is making something out of nothing and selling it.

—*Frank Zappa*

Italy is my true inspiration. The Artist is like a tree growing older, bent by the weight of its fruit, it presses always closer to the maternal womb that gave it birth. Despite everything, thirty years and more of America have succeeded only in making more solid and firm the Latin structure of my nature.

—*Joseph Stella*

Cinema

Proverb

Art consists in concealing art.

Voices

Charlie Chaplain used his ass better than any other actor. In all of his films his ass is practically the protagonist. For a comic, the ass has incredible importance.

—*Roberto Benigni*

It's too bad I'm not as wonderful a person as people say I am, because the world could use a few people like that.

—*Alan Alda*

It is only when I am doing my work that I feel truly alive.

Even if I set out to make a film about a filet of sole, it would be about me.

I'm embarrassed to confess, no, I don't go to the movies much. I've never gone much. As a boy in Rimini, they let me go to the movies once a week.

When, as a young man, I went to *Cinecitta* and saw the directors filming, I admired their power—to shout, scream, make beautiful actresses weep—I remember in particular having seen Blasetti make the very beautiful and very famous Isa Pola cry—but I also found them boorish, overbearing, vulgar, arrogant.

My films are not for understanding. They are for seeing.

—*Federico Fellini*

I wanted to glorify the average man, not the guy at the top, not the politician, not the banker, just the ordinary guy whose strength I admire, whose survivability I admire. Guys like Gary Cooper.

—*Frank Capra*

In an America that has lost touch with family life, *The Godfather* book and *The Godfather* films emphasized the importance of family, the idea of fidelity to family and vengeful reaction to those who are disloyal to family.

—*Gay Talese*

I always say this; learn how to read, learn how to read. Out loud. And e-nun-ci-ate pro-per-ly. And give it from here and from here. People just read sometimes. You know they just, "Zuck-a-zuck-a-zuck-a-zuck-a-zuck-a . . ." But you've got to give a little bit more, "ZUCK-A-ZUCK-AAAA.

—*Ernest Borgnine*

When such a great actor [Vittorio Gassman] dies, a guiding light is missing in the international community. I am Catholic and I have Italian origins: my mother Rose loved Italian movies and theater, and she taught me to follow them.

My limo just conked out. It just stopped in Santa Monica. Those things happen to me all the time.

They dyed my hair gray for a part I was playing. They actually bleached it and when it hits the sun it just goes blond. I actually like it.

The actor becomes an emotional athlete. The process is painful—my personal life suffers.

—*Al Pacino*

Acting is not that far from mental disease: An actor works on splitting his character into others. It is like a kind of schizophrenia.

—*Vittorio Gassman*

Art depends on luck and talent.

—*Francis Ford Coppola*

I feel like a father toward my old films. You bring children into the world, then they grow up and go off on their own. From time to time you get together, and it's always a pleasure to see them again.

Actors are like cows. You have to lead them through a fence.

Cinema today should be tied to the truth rather than logic . . . The rhythm of life is not made up of one steady beat; it is, instead, a rhythm that is sometimes fast, sometimes slow . . . There are times when it appears almost static . . . I think that through these pauses, through this attempt to adhere to a definite reality—spiritual, internal, even moral— there springs forth what today is more and more coming to be known as modern cinema, that, a cinema which is not so much concerned with externals as it is with those forces that move us to act in a certain way and not in another.

One of the themes of the film is to examine the myth of objectivity . . . I never think in terms of this kind of conflict: between the individual and the mass. I'm not a sociologist. I never make a political thesis. I would prefer it if something like this comes out of it. If I put a character against a landscape, there is naturally a relationship.

—Michelangelo Antonioni

See, lately—I don't know why—action movies have become like the movie business's equivalent of *The Hunchback of Notre Dame*. Just as Quasimodo was the ugly duckling in literature, action films have become the sore spot for critics. In the old days, people talked about biblical scenarios of action films. The Bible is action-packed. The Koran is action-packed. Even Buddha had a few moments of suspense in his life. Yet, when we make action movies now, we're considering moneymaking machines with no esoteric worth, and that's not true at all. There's a lot of artistry that goes into what we do. I tend to think of action movies as exuberant morality plays in which good triumphs over evil.

—*Sylvester Stallone*

After that movie [*Patton*] I feel so many things. I feel patriotism. I feel nationalism. He was so focused and disciplined. He's a true leader, and I would be proud to fight for him.

—*Mike Piazza*

Employ in everything a certain casualness which conceals art and creates the impression that what is done and said is accomplished without effort and without its being thought about.

—*Baldassare Castilione*

I love this game. I am so pleased that we are all so dedicated to mankind—unlike show business, where there you have egomaniacs and you have power mongers and you have elitists.

—*Sonny Bono*

I couldn't get any jobs, and when that happens, you get so humble it's disgusting. I didn't feel like a man anymore—I felt really creepy. I was bumping into a wall and saying, "Excuse me."

—*Joe Pesci*

I loved *The Godfather*. I thought that was the best interpretation of our life that I've ever seen.

I left that movie [*The Godfather*] stunned. I mean, I floated out of the theater. Maybe it was fiction, but for me, then, that was our life. It was incredible. I remember talking to a multitude of guys, made guys, who felt exactly the same way.

—*Sammy "The Bull" Gravano*

And all the time I was a farmer at heart, and I still am. When I am working I got to bed at nine-thirty and get up at five. Honest, I really believe I was happier when I slept on a bench in Central Park than during all the years of the "perfect-lover" stuff.

—*Rudolph Valentino*

You know, [Sinatra's] the idol. A great Italian American, a great American, and a great actor. There will never be another him. He was the original.

—*Martin Scorsese*

Music

Proverb

Music is an enticement to love.

Voices

When a Bing Crosby movie came to Steubenville [Ohio] I would watch all day. That's how I learned to sing, 'cause it's true I don't read a note. I learned by Crosby.

—*Dean Martin*

❧

I never think about my voice. . . . It's just been there since I was born.

—*Mario Lanza*

I would say that half the population of the United States over the age of forty was conceived while their parents were listening to [Frank Sinatra's] records. He played a great romantic role in the country. Sinatra got the blood flowing.

—*Gore Vidal*

I feel that you must compose when you have to compose, and not just when you want to. Unless it's a necessity, it's not worth trying. It's a gift from God, and if God wants you to compose he tells you. At the moment, God isn't paying me much attention.

—*Gian Carlo Menotti*

I once referred to the music department at Universal as a salt mine. But it was a good salt mine, and younger composers in film today do not have access to that kind of on-the-job training. Being on staff there I was called upon to do everything. I mean, *everything*.

—*Henry Mancini*

Frank Sinatra was the alpha and the omega of it all, the most influential singer and performer of all time. He will be sorely missed.

—*Tony Orlando*

Ain't that a kick in the ass? An old guy like me feeling like a kid again. But that's precisely the case. To allow my name to be mentioned in the same breath as the masters is not something I'm comfortable with.

—*Billy Joel*

Always loved music. I always loved singing, and fortunately, I still do.

Brooklyn—that's where it all started. We didn't have to contend with rock and roll back then, and when it came, I still didn't contend with it.

—*Julius La Rosa*

The audience knows I'm not going to do anything after all these years to upset them.

—*Perry Como*

I don't concentrate on projecting a high B with the thought that there's a high D coming right after it. I just sing.

—*Anna Moffo*

[Vic Damone's] all-around best performances are unquestionably his work today. He's still got those pipes, not at all rusted with the years, and he appears to know more about what to do with them.

—*Frank Sinatra*

The most brutal, ugly, degenerate, vicious form of expression it has been my displeasure to hear.

—*Frank Sinatra on rock 'n' roll at the time of Elvis Presley*

To this day I could probably sing everything that I've recorded in its original key. And my range is very broad. I could go from a low C if I really wanted to, up to an A flat. That's a flat above the scale.

—*Bobby Rydell*

. . . at the age of nine, my father had me singing *La Vie en Rose* in French, and *Siboney* in Spanish at the Steel Pier with my accordion. What's more, he was a fanatical country music fan.

—*Connie Francis*

My brother Leon started it all. He played the piano. In school they made me leader of the orchestra because I played the violin, but I followed Leon and the boys in his jazz band around. I wasn't making it with the violin because I was playing all of the "long hair" stuff.

There's nothing like walking out and watching the people get turned on. Nothing in the world could replace it.

—*Louis Prima*

Any subject is good for opera if the composer feels it so intently he must sing it out.

—*Gian Carlo Menotti*

The artist who boasts he is never nervous is not an artist—he is a liar.

—Enrico Caruso

I love to sing. I have the best job in the world.

—Salvatore Licitra

La Famiglia

Proverbs

How poor is a home without a woman!

Neither marriage nor war will go away once begun.

May my name be lost in your home.

Voices

In a big family the first child is kind of like the first pancake. If it's not perfect, that's okay, there are a lot more coming along.

—*Antonin Scalia*

The Italian family is a stronghold in a hostile land: within its walls and among its members, the individual finds consolation, help, advice, provision, loans, weapons, allies, and accomplices to aid in his pursuits. No Italian who has a family is ever alone. He finds in it refuge in which to lick his wounds after a defeat, or an arsenal and a staff for his victorious drives.

—*Luigi Barzini*

A man who has raised quintuplets has had enough of babies.

—*Franco Diligenti*

[My father] never worked a fuckin' day in his life. He was a rolling stone; he never provided for the family. He never did nothin'. He never earned nothin'. And we never had nothin'.

—*John Gotti*

Never have children, only grandchildren.

—*Gore Vidal*

Sometimes I question how I got to be the way I am. I had a great mother and father. I don't know how I got to be the way I am. No emotion. No feeling. Like fuckin' ice.

—*Sammy "The Bull" Gravano*

I watched a small man with thick calluses on both hands work fifteen and sixteen hours a day. I saw him once literally bleed from the bottoms of his feet, a man who came here uneducated, alone, unable to speak the language, who taught me all I needed to know about faith and hard work by the simple eloquence of his example.

A lot of my stories about the old days, they're delicious and funny, but . . . Every time I recall the early days, it's painful—painful because you're summoning up the terribly, terribly difficult life of my parents. And it's painful because I didn't realize at the time how hard it was for them.

I talk and talk and talk, and I haven't taught people in fifty years what my father taught me by example in one week.

—*Mario Cuomo*

My grandmother could have been a character in a fable herself. She was an old peasant woman; she was capable of great tenderness. She was an old, tall, thin woman with many petticoats.

—*Federico Fellini*

I also remember the holidays when all the relatives would gather at my grandfather's house and there'd be tables full of food and homemade wine and music. Women in the kitchen, men in the living room and kids, kids everywhere. I must have a half million cousins, first, second, and some who aren't even related, but, what did it matter. And my grandfather would sit in the middle of it all grinning his mischievous smile, proud of his family and how well his children had done.

—*Paul Parillo*

I began playing baseball on a vacant lot in San Francisco with the other kids in my neighborhood when I was about ten years old. In those days, I preferred almost anything to working on my father's fishing boat or cleaning it up when the fishing day was over. I hated the smell. My father looked on baseball in much the same way as I did on fishing.

—*Joe DiMaggio*

My father was a strong man, however, and I suppose I naturally enough learned to admire strength.

—*Charles Atlas*

Some of my earliest memories were walking in the street, holding his hand next to my cheek, just loving his presence. He was a very sweet, warm father.

—*Alan Alda*

A don is like your father and mother and God all rolled into one. He is your life. He is the head of your family. You owe him everything. You owe him the breath out of your lungs, your life, your soul, your religion.

—*Vincent Teresa*

Exactly what my father, who lacked most qualities that made a proverbial American, believed had attracted him to the United States, I never discovered. We never talked about it.

—*Luigi Barzini*

My mother gave me my drive but my father gave me my dreams.

—Liza Minnelli

As the father of a family, I was like the head of state. I too had to maintain internal order. I too had to conduct foreign affairs with other families.

—Joseph Bonanno

[*The Sopranos* is] a family show—it's about a mother, a son, an uncle, a wife and children, and all the ramifications, and then the guy's job, which happens to be hustler, con man, and a killer. It has nothing to do with gangsters—it's all about society.

—Dominic Chianese ("Uncle Junior")

All I know is that my relatives seemed happiest when they were crowded in a stuffy room noisy with chatter and children. Their passion for human company probably accounted for their relentless urge to produce children . . .

— Jerry Mangione

My father was always getting excited about something. It's genetically inside me somewhere.

—*Nicolas Cage*

My father was very strong. I don't agree with a lot of the ways he brought me up. I don't agree with a lot of his values, but he did have a lot of integrity, and if he told us not to do something, he didn't do it either.

—*Madonna Ciccone*

It's wishful thinking. I think everybody would like to have somebody that they could go to for justice, without going through the law courts and the lawyers. *The Godfather* was really, to me, a family novel, more than a crime novel.

—*Mario Puzo*

. . . I have so many children. Twenty-one to be exact . . . I'd better explain that my "children" are my dogs. And I couldn't love them more if I'd sired the whole litter. Friends have been known to say, "When I die, I want to come back as one of Liberace's dogs."

—*Liberace*

. . . my affection for Grandpa Alfonso goes beyond family ties and ethnic pride. More than anyone else, he showed me that with the right attitude and a little guts, life could be an adventure.

—*Al D'Amato*

I don't think my parents would be shocked about anything I did, because they're so laid-back.

—*Leonardo DiCaprio*

Is this my father? Why, look at him! Listen to him! He reads with an Italian inflection! He's wearing an Italian mustache. I have never realized it until this moment, but he looks exactly like a Wop. His suit hangs carelessly in wrinkles upon him. . . . And for the Lord's sake, will you look at his pants! They're not even buttoned in front. And, oh, damn, damn, damn, you can see those dirty old suspenders that he won't throw away. Say, mister, are you really my father? . . . You look exactly like one of those immigrants carrying a blanket. You can't be my father!

—*John Fante*

We were a real warm Italian family. Dinner was a real event in our house. It was a time for all of us to be together and talk about our day. Pop always got served first. And we never got up from the table until he got up.

—*Yogi Berra*

[My father] believed very strongly in his religion, and always taught me and my brother and sister to be honorable. He cobbled our shoes and made our leggings. He even made the tombstone for my mother's grave. There wasn't anything he couldn't do.

—*Peter Rodino*

The kind of childhood I had can make you or break you. I've had knocks, but I'm not sure it's not better to have them when you're young. At least it teaches you how to handle them when they come later.

—*Liza Minnelli*

My father had his bakery shop right where that orange car is. This is the street where my father was hit by a rock, because he was an Italian looking for work.

—*Connecticut governor Ella Grasso*

You know Sicilians are great liars, the best in the world. I'm Sicilian. My father was the world-heavy-weight champion of Sicilian liars. From growing up with him, I learned the pantomimes. There are seventeen different things a guy can do when he lies to give himself away. . . .

—*Quentin Tarantino*

. . . my parents. They spoke real bad Italian. But my grandparents spoke only Italian. So Grandma would teach me Italian songs.

—*Connie Francis*

For me my mother and father, until I was twenty-five, they were like furniture, they came with the house. I never thought of my mother as a woman, a girl with her own dreams and desires. And my dad he was just this guy that was a little older than me.

—*Bruce Springsteen*

From the beginning, I've been told, [my father] loved music and song, and as a boy he had a wonderful singing voice. He would often climb to the top of the mountains in Calabria and sing out to the whole valley below. Singing is a part of my heritage. I'm convinced it's in my blood, and that's why I'm a singer today.

—*Tony Bennett*

Food

Proverbs

Appetite comes with eating.

Gluttony kills more than the sword.

To make a proper salad: a wise man to season it, a miser for the vinegar, a spendthrift to pour the oil, and a madman to mix it.

The eyes eat before the stomach.

Hunger makes hard beans sweet.

Voices

Eating is not merely a material pleasure. Eating well gives a spectacular joy to life and contributes immensely to goodwill and happy companionship. It is of great importance to the morale.

—*Elsa Schiaparelli*

There are many miracles in the world to be celebrated and, for me, garlic is the most deserving.

—*Leo Buscaglia*

Of course I had been born in America and had lived here all my life, but, somehow it had never occurred to me that just being a citizen of the United States meant that I was an American. Americans were people who ate peanut butter and jelly on white bread that came out of plastic bags. Me? I ate pepper and egg sandwiches on Italian bread. I was *Italian!*

—*Paul Parillo*

Mangia, ricordo. [By eating I remember.] My memory seems more and more tied to the table, to a full table of good food and festivity; to the place of ritual and celebration in life. Yes, I believe in good food and festivity. Food is the medium of my remembrance, of my memory of Italy and family and of children at my table.

—Helen Barolini

Except the vine, there is no plant which bears a fruit of as great importance as the olive.

—Pliny the Elder

At first I just wanted to make enough wine to drink and pretend I was my grandfather. Even at that point, the idea of having your own wine, with your own label and your own family's name and your grandfather's picture on it was enough.

Once in a description I wrote, "Clemenza is in the kitchen, browning sausage in the olive oil." Mario crossed it out, with the note: "Clemenza is frying garlic in the olive oil . . . Gangsters don't 'brown,' gangsters 'fry.' "

—Francis Ford Coppola

Caffe Verona was named after the Italian city Verona, a favorite of CEO Howard Schultz. He wanted to capture the Italians' appreciation for coffee that he witnessed in the Italian cafes which included Italians sipping their coffee and eating a chocolate or pastry.

—*Cynthia Smith,*
Midwest operations manager for Starbucks

Anything you put in front of me. If I had to pick a favorite, I would say corn chips and guacamole. But I'll eat any damn thing you put out.

—*Janeane Garofalo*

I feast on wine and bread, and feasts they are.

I received twelve little cheeses some days ago and not only were they delicious, but good to look at.

—*Michelangelo Buonarotti*

Usually, before heading home, we went shopping in the nearby Italian streets for what Mother needed, then took the subway to Pennsylvania Station and the Long Island train. Commuters around us often sniffed the air and sometimes commented aloud about the odd suspicious smells emanating from our packages. They were the odor of fresh-roasted Italian coffee (unknown at the time in the United States, where the coffee smelled of nothing at all), strange spices, a rare white truffle, or Gorgonzola.

They eat the dainty food of famous chefs with the same pleasure with which they devour gross peasant dishes, mostly composed of garlic and tomatoes, or fisherman's octopus and shrimps, fried in heavily scented olive oil on a little deserted beach.

—*Luigi Barzini*

Imported pasta may look tempting, but our panel preferred American-made *Ronzoni*.

—*Editors of* Cook's Illustrated

I am grateful for the good fortune of having been born and raised in Bologna [Italy], for this city, with its heritage of great food. . . . Food in Bologna was such an integral part of one's life that being a skilled cook was nothing to boast about.

As a good Italian I never get tired of pasta. My daughters and my husband never get tired of pasta. My friends, when they come to dinner at my house, always expect pasta.

—*Biba Caggiano*

Venice is like eating an entire box of chocolate liqueurs in one go.

—*Truman Capote*

Life is a combination of magic and pasta.

—*Federico Fellini*

I have also loved good cooking and all the things that excite my curiosity.

I love strong tasting dishes: macaroni prepared by a good Neapolitan cook.

—*Giacomo Casanova*

Berlinzone, the land of the Basques, in a country called Bengodi, where. . . . there was a mountain made entirely of grated Parmesan cheese, on which lived people who did nothing but make macaroni and ravioli and cook them in capon broth. And then they threw them down, and the more of them you took, the more you had. And nearby ran a rivulet of white wine whose better was never drunk, and without a drop of water in it.

—*Bocaccio*

He who looks at magnitude
Is often mistaken.
A grain of pepper conquers
Lasagne with its strength.

—*Iacopone da Todi*

A great way to lose weight is to eat naked in front of a mirror. Restaurants will almost always throw you out before you can eat too much.

—*Frank Varano*

French cooking is formalized, technical, and scientific. Order Bearnaise sauce in 200 different French restaurants and you will get exactly the same sauce 200 times. Ask for Bolognese sauce in 200 different Italian restaurants and you will get 200 versions of *ragu*.

—*Enrico Galozzi*

Spaghetti can be eaten successfully if you inhale it like a vacuum cleaner.

—*Sophia Loren (attributed)*

[Italy's] food is twice blessed because it is the product of two arts, the art of cooking and the art of eating. While each nourishes the other, they are in no way identical accomplishments. The art of cooking produces the dishes, but it is the art of eating that transforms them into a meal.

I cannot imagine Italy without its vegetable stalls, filling ancient squares and animating dusty side streets with mounds of fabulous forms in purple, green, red, gold, and orange. In a land heavy with man's monuments, these are the soil's own masterworks.

The Italian comes to his table with the same open heart with which a child falls into his mother's arms, with the same easy feeling of being in the right place.

Today people seem to prefer cotton wadding to real bread, and the only ones still making [Italian olive-oil bread] are local bakers in a few small towns.

The good Italian cook is an improviser, whose performance is each time a fresh response to the suggestions of an inner beat.

La buona cucina is not an exercise in dexterity. It is an act of taste.

—*Marcella Hazan*

Whenever I think of pasta I think of my godfather, Tommaso, who returned to his native Abruzzi in Italy after he retired. . . . Tommaso ate macaroni in one form or another every day. He bought his pasta imported from Italy in twenty-five-pound wooden crates. When he finished with the crates, he would give them to me and I would make birdhouses out of them. Tommaso would eat two pounds of pasta at a sitting, yet he was never overweight and never went to a doctor or a dentist.

—*Edward Giobbi*

I guess I'm a little bit like the European chefs. I chop by hand, and I grate by hand, and I whisk by hand. They say a pianist's hands are his professional fortune. In the service of preparing a good meal, mine have been blistered while frying, scraped while grating, burned by getting something out of the oven, and cut while chopping, and they still work pretty well at the keyboard.

—*Liberace*

Etruscan Chianti that kisses you and bites you and makes you shed sweet tears.

—*Fulvio Testi*

If the first father of the human race was lost for an apple, what would he not have done for a plate of *tortellini*?

—*Bolognese poet*

Tortellini is more essential than the sun for Sunday, or love for a woman.

—*Gazetta di Bologna*

Leave the gun. Take the cannoli.

—*Mario Puzo*

La Mama

Proverb

Who has not children knows not what love is.

Voices

When you are a mother, you are never really alone in your thoughts. A mother always has to think twice, once for herself and once for her child.

—*Sophia Loren*

I don't know who's the mother and who's the daughter any more. She's got a heart bigger than the whole world, my daughter. She pays for everything. I wish to God every mother could say this . . .

> —*Antoinetta Ferraro,*
> *mother of Geraldine A. Ferraro*

Mamma showed me that she was the boss, and she taught me with painful clarity that either I behave or there would be real punishment. I chose the right way—I didn't want to face Mama's wrath again any time soon.

> —*Al D'Amato*

Italian mothers—if not working themselves—were at home cooking and cleaning, waxing, and ironing. They provided the children with love and the security of family. Though many Italian families were materially poor, they were psychologically and culturally very rich.

> —*Monsignor Geno Baroni*

My mother laughs, cries, screams, and carries on within five minutes with all the fervor of a real actress. I only need to watch her to get any inspiration I need.

—*Ben Gazzara*

. . . Mother organized all her things. She left three dresses wrapped in plastic, each with a little paper note attached by a safety pin. . . . With a dry matter-of-factness the notes announced: "First marriage," "Second marriage," "Third marriage."

—*Isabella Rossellini*

Mother was a shrewd and rigorous administrator of our limited resources. She managed to protect our European middle-class dignity; we had a cook and a maid, the least one could have at the time, and lived in a comfortable apartment.

—*Luigi Barzini*

I was born in a house near here. A midwife delivered me. My mother is ninety-three and lives in Florida. She still gives me orders: "You've got to do this song."

—*Vic Damone*

The most remarkable thing about my mother is that for thirty years she served the family nothing but leftovers. The original meal has never been found.

—*Calvin Trillin*

When I have babies, I don't want them brought up by a nurse. I'll either quit the movies entirely, or limit my pictures to one a year.

—*Annette Funicello*

My mother is, you know, a mother. She's always had very, very high objectives for me.

—*Rudolph Giuliani*

America

Proverbs

When in Rome, do as the Romans do.

He who leaves the old and takes the new knows what he leaves but does not know what he hath in view.

Voices

Before I came to America, I thought that the streets were paved with gold. When I arrived, I learned three things. First, the streets were not paved with gold. Second, the streets were not paved at all. Finally, I was expected to pave them. Only an immigrant can appreciate America.

—*Joseph Marchesi, 1919*

I am leaving but my heart remains. America is my Jupiter, Virginia my Venus.

I do not know what may happen when Sandy Hook disappears from my sight. But I know that wherever I go I shall always work for the well-being and progress of the country of my adoption.

—*Philip Mazzei*
friend of Thomas Jefferson

I am waiting for my case to come up
and I am waiting
for a rebirth of wonder
and I am waiting for someone
to really discover America

—*Lawrence Ferlinghetti*

Don't you get the idea I'm one of these goddamn radicals. Don't get the idea I'm knocking the American system . . .

—*Al Capone*

Ten years old, and a ready fist. I hated being poor, hated the ghetto, hated America.

My heart ached for him. Papa, illiterate Papa, ignorant of language and laws; running, dreaming of farms; running, lungs burning, from oven to oven; ten hours a day six days a week, a long-paddler running—for twelve lousy dollars. For this he came to America?

. . . I think when times are tough the people that survive are these ordinary people who are not afraid to show their feelings. They will survive. All the intellectuals will be knocked off or starve. The strength of America is in the kind of people who can plant a seed, sow the grass.

Take another look at the country that gave you a road to climb. Drink in its spirit; breathe deep its freedom. And take a special look at "We the People" who made this country great; people to whom weary souls can return again and again to commune and to draw, like Antaeus, another thankful of their courage and faith.

—*Frank Capra*

There was never a war on poverty. Maybe there was a skirmish on poverty.

—*Andrew Cuomo*

Grandpa Antonio Suraci really lived the "American dream," and took full advantage of the opportunities offered to him in his new country. He moved the family to a quieter neighborhood on Twelfth Street on the East Side between First and Second Avenues. It was here that my grandfather started a wholesale fruit-and-vegetable business catering to the pushcart owners. Every morning they congregated at his basement warehouse before sunrise to pick up the produce they'd sell all across downtown New York.

—Tony Bennett

. . . both gangs and organized crime have existed in America from early colonial days.

—Giovanni Schiavo

I am part of the process. My responsibility first is to listen and understand. I have a responsibility to protect the integrity of this process to create an inspiring and remarkable memorial and to have input from all stakeholders.

—*Anita F. Conti*

Once I went back to my native city and planned to stay there for a year or more. I locked the door of my studio in New York, said goodbye to all my friends, and went to the homeland where I have been born. What did I find? I was a foreigner in Italy. I could speak the language of course, but I couldn't think Italian. . . . I had planned to be away for a year but in four months I was on my return trip to the Bronx.

—*Attilio Piccirilli*

Until yesterday I was among folks who understood me. This morning I seemed to have awakened in a land where my language meant little more to the native (as far as meaning was concerned) than the pitiful noises of a dumb animal. Where was I to go? What was I to do? Here was the promised land. The elevated rattled by and did not answer. The automobiles and trolley sped by, heedless of me.

—*Bartolomeo Vanzetti*

The Constitution gives every American the inalienable right to make a damn fool of himself.

—*John Ciardi*

Everybody loves Italians! We're emotional, romantic, sentimental, and sing wonderfully; Italian men are all studs, and Italian women are all passionate. If we're sometimes a little slow-witted or vulgar, we have ways of taking care of snobs and getting revenge, and we don't bother with those not of our kind. We're a sweet and peppery people who stay to ourselves. And if you don't believe that, I'll break your arm.

—*John Mariani*

At the lunch hour I huddle over my lunch pail, for my mother doesn't wrap my sandwiches in wax paper, and she makes them too large, and the lettuce leaves protrude. Worse, the bread is homemade; not bakery bread, not "American" bread. I make a great fuss because I can't have mayonnaise and other "American" things.

—*John Fante*

We thought the way to become real Americans was to be more patriotic—be better Americans than anyone else. We flocked to American Legion oratorical contests and gave speeches on the flag and the Constitution. And we had to prove something. We had to march [like] the Italians on Columbus Day. We never realized that the WASPs never marched. Every day was their day.

—Monsignor Geno Baroni

An Italian, wasn't I? Then, it was silly for me to say I couldn't paint a landscape. "Your parents are Italian. I can tell by your name. Some of the greatest artists the world had ever known were Italian. No reason on earth why you can't paint a simple landscape."

—Jerry Mangione

Tonight, the daughter of an immigrant from Italy has been chosen to run for vice president in the new land my father came to love.

—Geraldine Ferraro

We will also have to remember that there is no absolute as to what one must be, feel, do, to be acceptably Italian American. We may be involved parochially in the search for ourselves, but we are also part of a larger search for the new American identity.

—*Giulio Miranda*

All my life I have been intrigued with a feeling or an impulse to know my ancestral roots, to know where and what I came from, to understand what makes me *me*. There is within my being an all-powerful longing to look back at my Italian [Sicilian] heritage to figure out what makes me *different* from others.

—*Philip di Franco*

I didn't cry. My heart didn't beat faster. But I was very glad I came. For the house, like the town and even Italy in general, confirmed my suspicions. I wasn't underneath *really* Italian. Neither was I just another good old red-blooded American. I was an Italian American—a unique breed, an identity in itself.

—*Anthony Mancini*

What disturbed [my mother] about the Americans . . . was their lack of interest in . . . books, poetry, history, and . . . their indifference to the virtues she cultivated: moderation, discipline, skepticism, prudence, thrift, patience, and understanding.

Like the America of all immigrants before and after him, his was not entirely a real country. It was mostly imaginary, a mosaic composed of all the virtues he believed Italy lacked, the perfections and improvements he had dreamed for his native land.

—Luigi Barzini

I feel that the Mafia is an incredible metaphor for this country.

—Francis Ford Coppola

Long before my mother had gone back to Italy both she and my step-father had realized the futility of their adventure. America had failed to offer its pot of gold. It had offered instead suffering, privation, and defeat. My stepfather's bondage in the piano factory literally crushed him for the rest of his life.

—Edward Corsi

. . . America, a nation whose freedom and well-being are inseparably tied to the freedom and well-being of other nations.

—Max Ascoli

Their version, magical and real at the same time, of an earthly paradise, lost and then found again: the myth of America.

—Carlo Levi

The United States is a nation of laws: badly written and randomly enforced.

—Frank Zappa

My one ambition and . . . daily prayer is to make beautiful the Capitol
of the one country on earth [America] where there is liberty.

—*Constantine Brumdi*

The right to food, shelter, and clothing at reasonable prices is as much
an inalienable right as the right to life, liberty, and the pursuit of
happiness.

—*Fiorello La Guardia*

Being
Italian American

Proverb

Marry a woman from your own neighborhood.

Voices

I have been an American for so long—fifty years—that I often forget I was born in Italy. When anyone refers to me as a foreigner, or as an Italian, I pretend that I haven't heard and I don't usually answer. Of course, I am an American. . . .

—*Atillio Piccirilli*

In my neighborhood you were either Italian or you were American. American meant you were anything *but* Italian. You had to be one or the other.

—*Joe Maselli*

[Mario Puzo] was usually very relaxed, with great stories and wisdom pouring out of him. It was fun just to be in his presence. He loved to eat, even though he knew he shouldn't. A little wine—not very much. And he was a New York Italian—couldn't really speak the Italian language and his opinions about food were basic—but enthusiastic.

—*Francis Ford Coppola*

My fuckin' father was born in New Jersey. He ain't never been in Italy his whole fuckin' life. My mother neither.

—*John Gotti*

. . . Every American was once an immigrant.

—*Fiorello La Guardia*

Above all, I look Italian. My clothes are Italian, but, more important, the expression on my face, the visible result of years of thinking Italian thoughts, is Italian.

—*Luigi Barzini*

There were many times when I wished that I had been born into a different family, a plain and simple family of impeccable American credentials—a no-secrets, nonwhispering, no-enemy-soldiers family that never received mail from POW camps, or prayed to a painting of an ugly monk, or ate Italian bread with pungent cheese.

—*Gay Talese*

"Public School No. 18: Paterson, New Jersey"
Miss Wilson's eyes, opaque
As blue glass, fix on me:
"We must speak English.
We're in America now."
I want to say, "I am American,"
But the evidence is stacked against me.

—*Maria Mazziotti Gillian*

Italian American women writers have explored the vital connections between being a woman and being ethnic in a world [America] which traditionally has valued neither.

—*Mary Jo Bona*

We were all born and raised no more than two blocks away from one another in South Philadelphia. We've known each other for years and it's just a ball working on stage with the other two guys, Frankie and Fabe.

[My brother] liked the atmosphere of downtown, where you could play with somebody next door or down the street, as opposed to out here, where you have to be literally driven everywhere. He just loved South Philly. And I love South Philly, it will always be in my heart.

—*Bobby Rydell*

If I walk out, I will say hello to fifteen or twenty people and they to me. "Hi, Sal. How are you? How's your father?" Like the old days. We're from different places in Italy, but we live in the same town.

—*Sal Calabrese,*
on Bensonhurst, Brooklyn

I have many Italian friends; I love Italian food; my girlfriend is half Italian; my daughter is Italian; and in order to feel good, I have to go to Italy once in a while. All this despite the fact that I was raised in the Bronx, with only a few Italians around.

—*Al Pacino*

No ten-generation Yankee family, like the Adamses, could ever make me feel inferior. I always said I'd rather be a pre-Columbian Roman than a post-Connecticut Yankee.

—*Carl Marzani*

Italian-American identity is in danger of being dissolved in a sea of inauthentic myths. Italian Americans shout, "We are!" but an army of those [in the media] who define them answer, "Look who's talking!" criminals, buffoons, racists and *cafoni* [peasants].

—*Richard Gambino*

As times change, you want to really revere your heredity, but you don't want to be a shrine . . . to light candles and kneel.

—*Kitty D'Alessio*

Everything always came back to being Italian . . .

Hollywood has robbed Italian Americans of a lot . . . what's being done to our culture is repulsive and it's got to stop.

—*Stanley Tucci*

I am proud to be Italian American.

—*David Chase*

I don't like the words *spick* and *nigger* because my people took the same kind of beating and I don't buy that stuff.

—*New York congressman Vito Marcantonio*

The term "Godfather" was never used by Italian criminals. Never. It was a term that I made up.

—*Mario Puzo*

The Godfather was a terrible, terrible movie, just pernicious. Despite its marvelous directorial techniques, it leads the audience to believe that organized crime is all Italian when, in fact, it includes every nationality. The film has made Italian Americans lose their dignity and feel embarrassed.

I consider my grandparents, as well as the many immigrants before and after them, to be the most courageous of people. It astounds me even to contemplate what it meant for them to leave behind everything they knew. They journeyed across the ocean without any idea of what they'd find on the other side, and none of them had ever ventured more than a few miles from the spot where they were born.

—*Tony Bennett*

Growing up as an Italian in New Jersey there were three staples in my childhood: a picture of the Pope in the living room, a pot of tomato sauce simmering on the stove, and Frank Sinatra playing in the background.

—*Robert Torricelli*

I have always been intensely proud that I am the son of Italian immigrants and that my Italian heritage helped make me the man I am.

—*Mario Cuomo*

Mob movies combine two things that Americans love: violence and a sense of family (the latter because so many of our own families are disintegrating). Unfortunately, this has come at the expense of Italian-American culture.

—*Dr. Joe Giordano*

Life is together. Fighting together. Playing ball together. You can't be some so-quiet guy in a room, jerking off by yourself.

—*Ralph Fasanella*

Italians in general take a bum rap. It's their tragedy. You know, 99.9% of Italian Americans are everything you should be in America. They're hardworking, they're doctors, lawyers, policemen, FBI agents, teachers. They take the rap for a handful of people.

—*Chicago policeman*

These people [who complain about negative Italian stereotypes] just want their fifteen minutes of fame.

—*Joe Pantoliano*

Next to Benny [Bugsy] Siegel, Meyer Lansky was the toughest guy, pound for pound, I ever knew in my whole life, and that takes in Albert Anastasia or any of them Brooklyn hoodlums or anybody you can think of.

—*Lucky Luciano*

[Italian families are] everything, it's what you feel about life.

—*Joe Mantegna*

You people married to Italian men, you know what it's like.

—*Geraldine A. Ferraro*

It's a family that's loaded with grudges and passion. We come from a long line of robbers and highwaymen in Italy, you know. Killers, even.

—*Nicolas Cage*

I didn't like that film [*The Godfather*]. What they did to the Italian people. There was no call for that. I know a lot of gangsters and they're not Italians.

—*Dean Martin*

Being born and raised in Brooklyn, I was always walking on concrete. When I walked on grass [in Westchester], it was like I moved to the country, which is what I wanted to do. Now with all the building [in the area], I call it "Times Square North."

—*Julius La Rosa*

Among the many stupid and ridiculous things I've done in my life, the stupidest was generally to scorn my Italian heritage. I deliberately refused to pick up any of the language. I looked down my nose at all the wonderful food.

—*Joe Barbera*

Rabiole
(Miscellany)

Proverbs

Either eat this soup or jump out this window.

Every law has a loophole.

He who scrubs the head of an ass wastes his time and efforts.

It's better to be cheated than stupid.

Voices

I like radio better than television because if you make a mistake on radio, they don't know. You can make up anything on the radio.

—*Phil Rizzuto*

A lawyer with a briefcase can steal more than a thousand men with guns.

—*Mario Puzo*

I'd rather find the good in people than the bad.

—*Congressman Peter Rodino*

When I sell liquor, it's called bootlegging; when my patrons serve it on silver trays on Lake Shore Drive, it's called hospitality.

—*Al Capone*

[Enrico] is the man I cook for and iron shirts for. How can I take him that seriously?

—*Laura Fermi*

❧

Okay, so I belong to the torn T-shirt school of acting, but I always wore a clean T-shirt under it.

—*Tony Franciosa*

❧

Politics is fascinating, vicious, unpredictable, demeaning, and it's very satisfying.

—*Mead Esposito*

❧

You better cut the pizza in four pieces because I'm not hungry enough to eat six.

How can you think and hit at the same time?

When you come to the fork in the road, take it.

—*Yogi Berra*

❧

He put his arm around me and he says that his name is Salvatore, like mine, that I'm his namesake, the "young Caesar." Then he starts quotin' Julius Caesar to me, in Latin, for chrissake. If he had somethin' nice to say to me, why the hell couldn't he have said it in English?

—*Lucky Luciano,*
on Maranzano

I don't like violence that much. I don't mind playing it, but I don't like watching it. Like, *A Clockwork Orange* I saw once, I could never watch it again. I get incredibly squeamish, believe it or not.

—*Michael Imperioli*

The real problem is what to do with the problem-solvers after the problems are solved.

—*Gay Talese*

"Pleeza no squeeza da banana."

—*Sung by Louis Prima*

I'm not worried about Italians. They're just a bunch of opera singers.

—*Franklin D. Roosevelt*

War is to man as maturity is to woman.

—*Benito Mussolini*

Religion is to women what salt is to pork. It preserves freshness and flavor.

—*Ignazio Silone*

Basically, I'm for anything that gets you through the night—be it prayer, tranquilizers, or a bottle of Jack Daniels.

—*Frank Sinatra*

Some men who claim to be exponents of Republican principles know as much about the teachings of Abraham Lincoln as Henry Ford knows about the Talmud.

—*Fiorello La Guardia*

In my senior year at Chafee [school] they said in the yearbook I would be the first woman mayor of Windsor Locks [CT]. I was horrified—politics! I mean, I aspired to something eminently greater.

—*Connecticut governor Ella Grasso*

I'm no thespian. But I'm more complex than I appear to be.

—*Sylvester Stallone*

Ai me! It is terrible to sing with one who does not bathe, but to be emotional over one who breathes garlic is impossible. . . . Tonight I must act better than I sing.

—*Enrico Caruso*

I asked a ref if he could give me a technical foul for thinking bad things about him. He said, of course not. I said, well, I think you stink. And he gave me a technical. You can't trust 'em.

—*Jimmy Valvano*

We are created in God's image, and God doesn't want to be a weakling.

All I want is to build a perfect race, a country of perfect human masterpieces.

—Charles Atlas

If I'm androgynous, I'd say I lean toward macho-androgynous.

—John Travolta

If I've made it a little easier for artists to work in violence, great! I've accomplished something.

—Quentin Tarantino

I think one of the reasons I'm popular again is because I'm wearing a tie. You have to be different.

—Tony Bennett

All I know I stole. If I saw you hold a cigaret a certain way, and I liked it, I would steal it from you.

If you call it a mistake, I guess it was being born of poor parents and raised in a tough neighborhood. If things had been different I might have gone to college and been sitting up there with Mr. Kefauver.

—Frank Costello

The only way I'd worry about the weather is if it snows on our side of the field and not theirs.

—Tommy Lasorda

The streets are safe in Philadelphia, it's only the people who make them unsafe.

—Frank Rizzo

I wouldn't have minded going to Vietnam. You get medals for killing people there.

—Sammy "The Bull" Gravano

Automatic simply means that you can't repair it yourself.

—Frank Capra

Advertising is the most fun you can have with your clothes on.

—Jerry Della Femina

They called me a rat. I take that as a compliment.

—Frank Serpico

Vote early and vote often.

—*Al Capone*

I hate music, especially when it's played.

—*Jimmy Durante*

A university is what a college becomes when the faculty loses interest in students.

You don't have to suffer to be a poet; adolescence is enough suffering for anyone.

—*John Ciardi*

I felt like poisoning a monk.

—*Umberto Eco, on why he wrote the novel* The Name of the Rose

History is the sum total of the things they're not telling us.

—*Don DeLillo*

Maybe the good Lord was just waiting for me to put on the pinstripes.

—Joe Torre

Heaven knows, I'm no sheik.

—Rudolph Valentino

Any American who is prepared to run for president should automatically, by definition, be disqualified from ever doing so.

Half of the American people have never read a newspaper. Half never voted for President. One hopes it is the same half.

I'm a born-again atheist.

A narcissist is someone better looking than you are.

A good deed never goes unpunished.

There is no human problem which could not be solved if people would simply do as I advise.

—Gore Vidal

You [Annabella Sciorra] speak Neapolitan, and I need a really bad, bad curse word.

—*David Chase*

I once shook hands with Pat Boone and my whole right side sobered up.

—*Dean Martin*

They couldn't put my real name, Robert Louis Ridarelli on the sign—there wouldn't be enough room!

—*Bobby Rydell*

I've given a lot of interviews; so, I don't trust what I say. I repeat myself. I try to remember what I've already said and what I still haven't said. For fear of repeating something I've already said, I invent other things.

—*Federico Fellini*

It's all crazy now, we're going too far the other way. When you see a model now they're all perfect, they're all tanned, they all have the same size breasts. They've all had surgery.

—*Giorgio Armani*

Thank the Lord for making me a Yankee.

—*Joe DiMaggio*

Sources

Alan Alda (1936–), actor

Vittorio Alfieri (1749–1803), poet

Dante Alighieri (1265–1321), author of *The Divine Comedy*

Giulio Andreotti (1919–), Italian politician

Mario Andretti (1940–), race car driver

Michelangelo Antonioni (1912–), film director

Eddie Arcaro (1916–1997), jockey

Pietro Aretino (1492–1556), poet

Giorgio Armani (1935–), clothing designer

Max Ascoli (1898–1978), publisher of *The Reporter*

Charles Atlas (Angelo Siciliano) (1892–1972), bodybuilding expert

Anne Bancroft (Anna Maria Italiano) (1931–), actor

Joseph Baretti (1719–1789), critic quoted in Boswell's *Life of Samuel Johnson*

Joe Barbera (1911–), creator of *Tom and Jerry*, *The Flintstones*, and *Scooby-Doo*

Helen Barolini (1925–), chef and cookbook author

Monsignor Geno Baroni (1930–1984), urban affairs, undersecretary of HEW

Luigi Barzini (1908–), author of *The Italians*

Pietro Belluschi (1899–1994), architect

Roberto Benigni (1952–), actor and director

Tony Bennett (Benedetto) (1926–), singer

Yogi Berra (1925–), professional baseball player and manager

Ugo Betti (1892–1954), poet and playwright, author of *Goat Island*

Giovanni Bocaccio (1313–1375), author of *The Decameron*

Raymond Bocci (n.d.), owner of L. Bocci and Sons Monuments in Colma, California, quoted in *Dream Streets* by Lawrence diStasi

Umberto Boccioni (1882–1916), Italian painter and sculptor

Hector Boiardi (1898–1985), chef, quoted in *Dream Streets* by Lawrence diStasi

Mary Jo Bona (n.d.), professor of Italian studies, University of Wisconsin

Jon Bon Jovi (John Francis Bongiori) (1962–), musician

Sonny Bono (1935–1998), singer and composer

Ernest Borgnine (1917–), actor

John Brucato (1904–), founder of San Francisco's Farmer's Market, quoted in *Dream Streets* by Lawrence diStasi

Constantino Brumidi (1805–1880), painter of frescoes in Capitol building, Washington, D.C.

Michelangelo Buonarotti (1475–1564), artist and sculptor

Leo Buscaglia (1924–1998), writer

Julius Caesar (102 or 100–44 B.C.), Roman dictator

Nicolas Cage (1964–), actor

Biba Caggiano (1937–), contemporary chef and cookbook writer

Guido Calabrese (1932–), Yale Law School dean

Sal Calabrese (n.d.), resident of Bensonhurst, Brooklyn, quoted in *The New York Times* on October 17, 2002

Joseph A. Califano, Jr. (1931–), attorney, former secretary of HEW

Al (Alphonse) Capone (1899–1947), Chicago boss of Colosimo family

Truman Capote (1924–1984), writer and actor

Frank Capra (1897–1991), film director

Jennifer Caprioti (1976–), professional tennis player

Frank Carlucci (1930–1987), former U.S. secretary of defense

Enrico Caruso (1873–1921), opera star

Benvenuto Cellini (1500–1571), Italian Renaissance artist

David Chase (DeCesare) (1945–), creator of *The Sopranos*

Sandro Chia (1946–), artist

Dominic Chianese (1934–), plays Uncle Junior in *The Sopranos*

Count Galleazzo Ciano (?–1945), son-in-law of Benito Mussolini

John Ciardi (1916–1986), writer

Madonna Ciccone (1958–), singer

Perry Como (1912–2001), singer

Anita F. Conti (n.d.), vice president of Lower Manhattan Development Corp., director of 9/11 rebuilding

Francis Ford Coppola (1934–), film director
Edward Corsi (1896–?), author of *In the Shadow of Liberty*
Gregory Corso (1930–2001), poet
Frank Costello (1891–1973), New York crime boss
Andrew Cuomo (1957–), politician
Mario Cuomo (1932–), former governor of New York
Kitty D'Alessio (1929–), business executive
Alfonse D'Amato (1937–), politician, former New York senator
Anthony J. D'Angelo (n.d.), author of *The Blue College Book*
Vic Damone (1928–), singer
Bobby Darin (1936–1973), singer
Leonardo da Vinci (1452–1519), artist
George T. Delacorte (1894–1991), publisher and philanthropist architect
Don DeLillo (1936–), writer
Jerry Della Femina (1936–), advertising executive
Vine Deloria, Jr. (1933–), political scientist
Robert De Niro (1943–), actor
Leonardo DiCaprio (1974–), actor
Philip Di Franco (n.d.), contemporary writer, author of *Italian Americans*
Joe DiMaggio (1914–1999), professional baseball player
Alfred Drake (1914–1992), actor
Jimmy Durante (1893–1980), entertainer
Leo Durocher (1905–1991), professional baseball manager
Umberto Eco (1932–), novelist

Meade Esposito (1909–?), Brooklyn Democratic Party leader

Fabio (Lanzoni) (1961–), model, appears on over 350 romance novel covers

Joe Falcon (1900–1965), musician

Giovanni Falcone (1939–1992), Italian government official

Ralph Fasanella (1914–), artist, quoted in *Dream Streets* by Lawrence diStasi

John Fante (1909–1983), writer, author of *Brotherhood of the Grape*

Federico Fellini (1920–1993), film director

Lawrence Ferlinghetti (1919–), poet

Enrico Fermi (1901–1954), Nobel Prize winner in physics

Salvatore Ferragamo (1898–1960), fashion designer and manufacturer

Antoinetta Ferraro (1915–), mother of Geraldine A. Ferraro

Geraldine A. Ferraro (1935–), politician, first woman to run for U.S. vice presidency

Frank Fontaine (1920–1978), actor

Tony Franciosa (1928–), singer

Connie Francis (Concetta Maria Franconero) (1938–), singer

Saint Francis of Assisi (1182–1226), founder of Franciscan order

Frank Frazetta (1928–), artist and illustrator of "Tarzan," "Buck Rogers," and "Flash Gordon"

Annette Funicello (1942–), Hollywood star, received her start on the *Mickey Mouse Club*

Galileo Galilei (1564–1642), Italian astronomer and physicist

Enrico Galozzi (n.d.), Italian gastronomic expert, quoted in Waverly
   Root's *The Food of Italy*
Julio Gallo (1938–1989), owner of Gallo Vineyards
Richard Gambino (n.d.), member of the Gambino family
James Gandolfini (1961–), star of *The Sopranos*
Frank M. Garafola (n.d.), writer
Joe Garagiola (1926–), professional baseball player and sportscaster
Janeane Garofalo (1964–), actor
Vittorio Gassman (1922–2000), film director
Ben Gazzara (1930–), actor
Alberto Giacometti (1901–1966), sculptor
A. Bartlett Giamatti (1938–1989), baseball executive and president
   of Yale University
Amadeo Peter Giannini (1870–1949), founder of Bank of Italy
Maria Mazziotti Gillan (1940–), contemporary poet
Edward Giobbi (1926–), painter and author of *Italian Family Cooking*
Dr. Joe Giordano (n.d.), coauthor of *Ethnicity and Family Therapy*
Rudolph Giuliani (1944–), former mayor of New York City
John Gotti, Sr. (1940–2002), don of Gambino family
Ella Grasso (1919–1981), former governor of Connecticut
Sammy "The Bull" Gravano (1945–), underboss of Gambino family
Francesco Guicciardini (1483–1540), historian and statesman
Marcella Hazan (1924–), chef and author of *Classic Italian Cooking*
Lee (Lido) Iacocca (1924–), business executive

Iacopone da Todi (?–1306), Italian poet

Michael Imperioli (1966–), plays the role of Christopher in *The Sopranos*

Silius Italicus (A.D. 25–101), Roman poet

Billy Joel (1949–), singer

Fiorello LaGuardia (1882–1947), former mayor of New York City

Frankie Laine (Francis Paul LoVechio) (1913–), singer

Julius LaRosa (1930–), singer

Tommy Lasorda (1926–), professional baseball manager

Luisa Leone (Mamma) (1873–1944), restaurateur

Carlo Levi (1902–1975), novelist

Liberace (1919–1987), musician and performer

Salvatore Licitra (1968–), opera tenor, debut at New York Metropolitan
    Opera, 2002

Gina Lollabrigida (1927–), actor

Vince Lombardi (1913–1970), professional football coach

Sophia Loren (Scicolone) (1934–), actor

Lucky Luciano (?–1962), boss of Genovese family

Salvador E. Luria (1912–1991), Nobel laureate in medicine

Niccolò Machiavelli (1469–1527), politician and author of *The Prince*
    and *The Art of War*

Anna Magnani (1908–1973), actress

Anthony Mancini (1939–), contemporary writer and journalist, quoted
    in *The New York Times* February 2, 1971

Henry Mancini (1924–1994), musical composer

Jerry Mangione (n.d.), author of *Mount Allegro*

Joe Mantegna (1947–), actor

Vito Marcantonio (1902–1954), politician and New York congressman

John Mariani, Jr. (1932–), wine executive

Marcus Valerius Martialis (A.D. 104), Roman writer

Dean Martin (1917–1995), singer

Tony Martin (1912–), actor

Carl Marzani (1912–), political activitist and writer

Joe Maselli (1924–), New Orleans businessman and Italian activist

Philip Mazzei (1730–1816), Italian statesman and friend of Thomas
    Jefferson

Cosimo de' Medici (1389–1464), Italian politician and banker

Gian Carlo Menotti (1911–), composer

Giovanni di Bicci de' Medici (1360–1429), founder of Medici banking
    business and father of Cosimo

Liza Minnelli (1946–), singer and actor

Giulio Miranda (n.d.), writer

Anna Moffo (1934–), opera star

A. J. Montanari (1917–), founder of school for emotionally disturbed
    children

Maria Montessori (1870–1953), educator

Alberto Moravia (1907–1990), novelist

Giovanni Morelli (1816–1891), art critic and Italian patriot

Willie Moretti (?–1951), member of Gambino family

Benito Mussolini (1883–1945), dictator and founder of Fascist movement

Tony Orlando (1944–), singer

Al Pacino (1940–), actor

Bruno Paglia (n.d.), author

Camille Paglia (1947–), author and critic

Achille Paladini (n.d.), founder of San Francisco fish business, quoted in
  Dream Streets by Lawrence diStasi

Joe Pantoliano (1951–), actor and cast member of *The Sopranos*

Paul Parillo (n.d.), co-owner of a family deli, La Cucina di Parillo in
  Amsterdam, New York

Jeno Paulucci (1918–), business tycoon and founder of Chun King Foods

Joe Pesci (1943–), actor

Petrarch (1304–1374), poet

Mike Piazza (1968–), professional baseball player

Attilio Piccirilli (1865–1945), sculptor

Rick Pition (1952–), professional basketball player and motivational
  author

Titus Maccius Plautus (250–184 B.C.), poet and author of *Miles Gloriosus*
  and *Captivi*

Pliny the Elder (A.D. 23–79), historian and author of *Natural History*

Marco Polo (1254–1324), explorer

Frank Pomilia (n.d.), California fisherman, quoted in *Dream Streets* by
  Lawrence diStasi

Rosa Ponselle (1897–1981), opera diva

Louis Prima (1910–1978), musician, actor

Mario Procacciono (1912–1995), politician, ran for mayor of New York City in 1969

Mario Puzo (1920–1999), novelist and author of *The Godfather*

Frank Rizzo (1920–1991), former mayor of Philadelphia

Phil Rizzuto (1818–), professional baseball player and sportscaster

Simon Rodia (1879–1965), sculptor and designer of Watts Towers

Peter Rodino (1909–), U.S. congressman, retired 1989

Franklin D. Roosevelt (1884–1945), thirty-second president of the United States

Isabella Rosselini (1952–), actor

Bobby Rydell (1942–), actor

Jacopo Sannazaro (1458–1530), poet

Susan Sarandon (1946–), actor

Vincent Sardi (1885–1969), owner of Sardi's Restaurant in New York City

Antonin Scalia (1936–), United States Supreme Court justice

Elsa Schiaparelli (1896–1974), fashion designer

Giovanni Schiavo (1898–1983), historian and writer

Martin Scorsese (1942–), film director

August Sebastiani (?–1980), head of Sebastiani Vineyards, quoted in *Dream Streets* by Lawrence diStasi

Frank Serpico (1936–), New York City detective

Cesare Siepi (1923–), opera star

Ignazio Silone (1900–1978), novelist

Frank Sinatra (1915–1998), singer

Paolo Soleri (1919–), architect of prototype town, Arcosanti, in Arizona

Bruce Springsteen (1949–), singer

Sylvester Stallone (1946–), actor

Frank Stella (1936–), artist

Joseph Stella (1877–1946), artist

Cornelius Tacitus (A.D. 55–120), Roman historian

Gay Talese (1932–), writer

Quentin Tarantino (1963–), film director

Vincent Teresa (n.d.), *sotto capo*, quoted in *The Italian Americans* by
    Andrew Rolle

Fulvio Testi (1593–1646), Italian poet

Robert Torricelli (1951–), politician, former U.S. senator

Arturo Toscanini (1867–1957), orchestra conductor

John Travolta (1954–), actor

Calvin Trillin (1935–), food writer

Stanley Tucci (1960–), actor

Joseph Valachi (1904–1971), member of Genovese family

Jerry Vale (1932–), actor

Rudolph Valentino (1895–1926), actor

Jimmy Valvano (1946–1993), basketball coach, sportscaster, motivational
    writer

Bartolomeo Vanzetti (1888–1927), labor leader, executed for murder

Frank Varano (1971–), contemporary musician

Edgard Varese (1885–1965), musician

Marcus Terentius Varro (116–27 B.C.), Roman scholar and author

Giorgio Vasari (1511–1574), art historian

Ken Venturi (1931–), professional golfer and sportscaster

Gore Vidal (1925–), writer

Harry Warren (Salvatore Guaragna) (1893–1981), musical composer

Richard Zamboni (1933–), son of Frank Zamboni (1901–1988),
    inventor of ice rink surfacing machine

Frank Zappa (1940–1993), musician